SEDUCTION
CODE
DEMYSTIFIED

How To Become a Chick Magnet

DON GIOVANNI

Pickup Artists Anonymous

DISCLAIMER

This book provides suggestions only and how the reader uses it is their choice. The authors / publishers are not liable for inappropriate use of the information by the reader.

CONTENTS

1 PREAMBLE TO THE SEDUCTION CODE

This book comprises top seduction advice tailored for men. It has been meticulously compiled after extensive research, gathering pearls of wisdom from seasoned pickup artists. I am confident that this book has the potential to revolutionize any man's romantic fortunes.

In today's digital age, there is an abundance of seduction advice available online. However, amidst the plethora of information, only a handful of techniques truly yield success in enhancing one's appeal to women.

The most effective dating and seduction advice often emanates from online forums and specialized books dedicated to improving one's technique and inner confidence. These resources prioritize the development of self-assurance as a foundational aspect of seduction.

I firmly believe that the insights contained within this collection of seduction strategies can empower men to achieve unprecedented success in their romantic endeavors, regardless of their physical appearance or financial status. Key aspects addressed in this book include:

- Understanding the intricacies of female psychology to initiate conversations that lead to attraction.

- Mastering the art of approaching women with the self-assuredness they seek in a potential partner.

- Enhancing conversational skills to establish rapport effortlessly with women.

- Identifying pitfalls to avoid when pursuing a woman of interest.

- Unveiling the universal principles that enable any man to successfully connect with women.

- Essential strategies for achieving genuine success in romantic pursuits.

- Recognizing the types of women who are most receptive to male approaches.

Additionally, the book delves into common mistakes men make that either repel or captivate women's interest.

Discovering effective seduction advice is straightforward when one knows where to look. It is advisable to conduct thorough research when seeking dating guidance for men. Some recommendations stem from professionals who have personally tested and refined the techniques outlined in their guides, ensuring their efficacy.

For most men, cultivating inner confidence forms the cornerstone of successful seduction. Embracing one's attractiveness and projecting self-assurance when approaching women are fundamental principles for achieving romantic success.

The Seduction Code

The Seduction Code is the art by which a man knowingly lures or attracts a woman. It is the process through which one can tempt or charm a lady into falling for them.

Seduction is often associated with the application of sexual desire, with the primary goal being to charm or attract a lady into doing what the seducer desires. It is not a prerequisite for men to be in love with the women they seduce.

Sexual attractiveness serves as the primary motivation for a man to seduce a woman whom he finds sexually appealing.

Different techniques can be employed to seduce the women one is attracted to. The choice of techniques depends on the woman's traits and the specific situation.

Several social behavior theorists assert that seduction is a unique form of persuasion. Some even describe seduction as a power reliant on psychological mastery rather than intellectual appeals, money, or fame.

Creating an artificial situation is necessary if one desires to sleep with a woman they are attracted to. This entails enticing the woman so that she cannot resist falling into lust.

It is crucial to enhance one's sexual attractiveness through various means, as this is key to successful seduction. If a woman does not find you sexually attractive, she is unlikely to sleep with you.

It is important to note that most women are selective about the men they sleep with. Unlike men, for whom sex may be more of a necessity, it is often a choice for women. Consequently, men require more tips and advice on seduction compared to women. Many men lack the know-how to engage in meaningful conversations with women and may not understand what topics to broach or avoid to create attraction.

Seduction techniques vary for different women. While one technique may work for a particular woman, it may not be effective for another. Understanding the personality and mindset of the woman is crucial in determining which techniques to employ.

In this book, readers will learn effective ways and techniques to seduce women. Additionally, they will discover what actions to avoid when attempting to seduce a woman.

2 UNDERSTANDING THE TYPES OF LOVE

Numerous theories have been posited by psychologists and researchers to elucidate the complexities of love. Among them, four major theories have emerged to shed light on the phenomena of liking, love, and emotional attachment.

Distinction Between Liking and Loving

Psychologist Zick Rubin put forth the notion that romantic love comprises three essential elements: attachment, caring, and intimacy. Attachment pertains to the longing for care, approval, and physical closeness with the other individual. Caring involves valuing the needs and happiness of the other person as much as one's own. Intimacy encompasses the sharing of thoughts, desires, and feelings with the other individual.

Drawing from this conceptualization, Rubin developed a questionnaire to gauge attitudes toward others. His findings indicated that these scales of liking and loving provided validation for his conception of love.

Contrast Between Compassionate and Passionate Love

According to psychologist Elaine Hatfield and her colleagues, there exist two fundamental types of love:

compassionate love and passionate love.

Compassionate love is characterized by mutual respect, attachment, affection, and trust. Typically, it arises from feelings of shared understanding and mutual respect.

On the other hand, passionate love is marked by intense emotions, sexual attraction, anxiety, and affection. When these intense feelings are reciprocated, individuals often feel elated and fulfilled, but unreciprocated love can lead to feelings of despondency and despair. Hatfield suggests that passionate love is transient, typically lasting between 6 and 30 months.

Hatfield posits that passionate love emerges under circumstances where cultural expectations encourage falling in love, when the person aligns with your idealized image of a partner, and when you experience heightened physiological arousal in their presence.

Ideally, passionate love evolves into compassionate love, which is more enduring. While most people aspire to relationships that blend the security and stability of compassionate love with the intensity of passionate love, Hatfield suggests that such unions are rare.

Color Wheel Model of Love

In his 1973 book 'The Colors of Love', John Lee likened styles of love to the color wheel. Like how three primary colors form the basis for all other colors, Lee proposed three primary styles of love: (1) Eros, (2) Ludus, and (3) Storge.

Expanding on the color wheel analogy, Lee suggested that just as primary colors can be combined to produce complementary colors, the three primary styles of love can be combined to generate nine secondary love styles. For instance, blending Eros and Ludus results in Mania, or obsessive love.

The 6 Styles of Love

Three primary styles:

1. Eros – Love for an idealized person
2. Ludus – Love viewed as a game
3. Storge – Love akin to friendship

Three secondary styles:

4. Mania (Eros + Ludus) – Obsessive love
5. Pragma (Ludus + Storge) – Realistic and pragmatic love
6. Agape (Eros + Storge) – Selfless love

Triangular Theory of Love

Psychologist Robert Sternberg proposed a triangular theory of love, positing that love comprises three components: intimacy, passion, and commitment. Different combinations of these components yield various types of love. For instance, intimacy and commitment combined result in compassionate love, while passion and intimacy produce passionate love.

According to Sternberg, relationships founded on two or more elements are more enduring than those rooted in a single component. Sternberg coined the term consummate love to denote a blend of intimacy, passion, and commitment. Although this form of love is the most robust and enduring, Sternberg suggests it is relatively rare.

Romantic Love

Romantic love is characterized by a surge of chemicals in the brain, evoking feelings of emotional exhilaration, passion, and elation when you are with your partner.

The age-old adage about love being blind aptly captures the essence of romantic love. Those experiencing romantic love often desire constant companionship with their partner and may overlook faults, conflicts, or even instances of abuse.

Infatuation is a component of romantic love. Scientific literature suggests that most individuals cannot sustain such intense emotional highs for extended periods, such as years on end.

As the infatuation or romantic love phase of a relationship wanes, a sense of disillusionment may set in. Spouses may become more critical of each other, easily irritated by things that previously did not bother them, exhibit less patience, and display indifference towards each other's wants and feelings.

Also Known As: Puppy love, sexual love, having a crush, infatuation.

Importance of Love

Often, we devote most of our time to tending to our physical needs. We ensure our bodies are nourished, clean, clothed, exercised, and rested. We also prioritize intellectual stimulation and entertainment. Yet, amidst these necessities, we often overlook the most vital need of all – love.

Admittedly, as a society, we do not disregard love. Popular media incessantly highlights the importance of attracting "love" and dictates how we should present ourselves. However, the desire to be loved pales in comparison to the profound emotional need to love someone else.

The innate urge to love and care for others is ingrained in us biologically. It is what compels parents to sacrifice sleep, sustenance, and sanity while raising their children. It is what drives individuals to endanger themselves to rescue others from both natural disasters and human threats. This primal need underpins the functioning of human society, both on an individual level and a societal scale.

Loving others enables us to prioritize their needs and desires over our own. We are willing to toil harder and longer, even in jobs we detest, to provide for those we love. We endure otherwise intolerable circumstances to offer care to our loved ones, whether they are young or old.

Understanding Desire

At the heart of the art of seduction lies a profound comprehension of desire—the elemental force that propels human attraction and ignites the flames of romantic longing. To truly become a master of seduction, one must embark on a voyage through the intricate depths of desire, unraveling its mysteries and wielding its power with finesse and sophistication. Let us embark on a captivating journey to unravel the essence of desire and its pivotal role in the mesmerizing dance of seduction between individuals.

Desire, in its essence, is a potent force that springs

forth from the core of human nature. It encompasses a kaleidoscope of primal instincts, emotional yearnings, and psychological cravings, propelling individuals on a quest for connection, intimacy, and fulfillment in their relationships. It is the magnetic pull that draws souls together in a tantalizing embrace, beckoning them to explore the depths of passion and longing.

Understanding the intricacies of desire requires a keen awareness of the psychological triggers that ignite its flames. These triggers, rooted in the subconscious mind, wield a profound influence on perceptions of desirability and attraction. From physical allure and confidence to charisma and social status, each trigger holds the key to unlocking the hidden chambers of desire, igniting a fervent blaze of passion within the hearts of those who succumb to its allure.

Beneath the surface of conscious awareness lies a realm of unconscious desires—a realm where hidden longings and forbidden fantasies lay dormant, waiting to be awakened. The art of seduction lies in skillfully tapping into these hidden depths, arousing passions, and kindling a primal fire within the object of desire. It is a delicate dance of unveiling the forbidden fruit of desire, luring the senses into a whirlwind of intoxicating ecstasy.

Emotional connection serves as the fertile soil in which desire takes root and blossoms into a profound bond between individuals. By cultivating genuine rapport, empathy, and understanding, seducers can forge deep emotional connections that resonate with the deepest desires of their target, paving the way for seductive conquests that transcend the boundaries of ordinary experience.

The power of anticipation is a potent aphrodisiac that fuels the flames of desire, tantalizing the senses with the promise of what lies beyond the realm of possibility. Seducers adeptly harness the power of anticipation, weaving a seductive narrative that captivates the imagination and leaves their target yearning for more. It is the art of leaving a trail of breadcrumbs that leads to the ultimate prize—a prize that beckons with the irresistible allure of forbidden pleasure.

Seduction is an inherently sensual and erotic dance—a dance that taps into the primal urges and carnal desires that lie dormant within us all. Through subtle gestures, seductive glances, and suggestive innuendos, seducers awaken the dormant passions of their target, stirring a primal hunger for intimacy and pleasure that cannot be denied.

Mystery and intrigue serve as potent catalysts for desire, shrouding the seducer in an aura of enigmatic allure. By leaving room for curiosity and ambiguity, seducers draw their target into a captivating dance of seduction, fueling their desire to unravel the mysteries that lie beneath the surface.

Flirtation is the playful exchange of seductive banter— a delicate interplay of wit, charm, and innuendo that titillates the senses and ignites the flames of desire. Through subtle cues and suggestive gestures, seducers tease and tantalize their target, leaving them craving more of their intoxicating presence.

Creating an irresistible aura of allure and magnetism is essential in the art of seduction. Seducers cultivate an aura of mystery and allure that draws their target into their orbit, leaving them utterly captivated by their presence. It is the art of projecting desire and magnetism, drawing others into the irresistible allure of seductive temptation.

Despite the fiery passions that fuel the flames of seduction, it is imperative to always honor the principles of consent and respect. True seduction is a dance of mutual attraction and desire, built on a foundation of trust, communication, and respect for the boundaries of both parties involved.

In essence, the foundations of seduction are rooted in a deep understanding of desire—the primal force that drives human attraction and fuels the seductive pursuit of intimacy and connection. By mastering the art of seduction and harnessing the power of desire, one can unlock the secrets of captivating the hearts and minds of others, forging deep and meaningful connections that transcend the boundaries of ordinary experience.

3 BECOME A CHICK MAGNET

Have you ever pondered over ways to attract women to you? If so, you may have inadvertently delved into the realm of psychology. There exists a branch of study known as social psychology dedicated to uncovering the types of men most favored by women. Researchers in this field do not focus on materialistic factors, such as wealth, that draw women to men; rather, they delve into the psychological dynamics of the seduction process.

Recent research conducted in Japan and Britain has shed light on the factors influencing seduction, revealing that it is not just about how a guy smells or looks. The study suggests that women are cognizant of the fact that good looks alone may not make for a suitable long-term partner. Subconsciously, they recognize that handsome men may be better suited for short-term relationships. Furthermore, the study indicates that women's preferences in men fluctuate with their menstrual cycle. During ovulation, approximately two weeks after their periods, women tend to prefer masculine men, while on other days, they lean towards more feminine-looking men. This fluctuation is attributed to the heightened hormonal levels during ovulation.

General Rules of Creating Attraction

There are numerous general rules for creating attraction. To captivate and enchant any woman, one must exude outward confidence and maintain a calm and composed demeanor. It is crucial not to display temper, as it can tarnish the gentlemanly image you have cultivated and work against the seduction process.

Attracting and seducing women is not a daunting task if you are mindful of your words and actions in their presence. The entire process hinges on your thoughts and mindset, with your mind playing a pivotal role in seduction.

Let us delve into how it works. If you believe you possess the ability to attract and seduce alluring women, repeatedly affirm to yourself that you possess the power and confidence to charm them. Merely uttering these affirmations is not sufficient; you must genuinely believe in them. By consistently repeating this affirmation, it becomes ingrained in your psyche, leading to an increase in your confidence levels. Over time, you will find that women are drawn to you irresistibly, unable to resist your allure.

Develop Powerful Self-Confidence

Developing powerful self-confidence is crucial for success in various aspects of life, including relationships. One of the simplest methods to achieve this is by regularly using affirmations.

Affirmations are statements about yourself written in the present tense, describing the ideal version of yourself that you aspire to become. They have a profound impact on your subconscious mind and, based on my experience, they can manifest into reality. It is advisable to read them a couple of times a day, especially before interacting with women.

When crafting affirmations, ensure they are written in the present tense. For instance, instead of saying, "I will be relaxed and comfortable," say, "I am relaxed and comfortable." Additionally, make them positive affirmations, focusing on what you want to embody rather than what you want to avoid. For example, say, "I am a winner," rather than "I'm not a loser."

While it is beneficial to create affirmations tailored to your personal goals and aspirations, here are some examples to get you started:

- I am friendly.
- I am fun-loving.
- I am approachable.
- I am interesting.
- I am clever.
- I am a leader.
- I am challenging.

- I am successful in all that I do.
- I can attract any woman I desire.
- I know my purpose.
- I am confident in who I am.
- I am an attractive man.
- I have a powerful reality.
- I am cool, calm, and collected.

By consistently reinforcing these positive affirmations, you can cultivate powerful self-confidence and project an irresistible aura of confidence and charisma.

You can also write them out as a paragraph:

In my world and life, I exude attractiveness and intrigue. People are drawn to me; they seek out my company. I possess a genuine curiosity about others, eagerly seeking connections with fun, positive, and interesting individuals.

To gauge their effectiveness, simply read the above paragraph aloud and notice if you feel uplifted! It is essential to counterbalance the negativity that surrounds many of us, and affirmations offer an effective method to achieve this.

Within our brains, there exists a particular unconscious region that operates ceaselessly, 24/7. This part of the brain dutifully follows any commands it receives. It is imperative to program your unconscious mind to align with the instructions you provide. By consistently affirming to your unconscious mind that you possess the qualities that drive women wild, you will notice a surge in confidence and sex appeal. Through repetition, you will subconsciously internalize the belief that you are a magnet for women's attention, and nothing can hinder their attraction to you.

Confidence is paramount in the seduction process. Typically, a man exudes confidence when he is successful and content in life. Men who have achieved fulfillment in these two crucial aspects are not desperate for female attention. They remain unfazed by rejection, knowing that with each closed door, another opens. It is their happiness and success that equip them to handle rejection with ease. In essence, a man earns the title of "chick magnet" when he is both accomplished and content in his own life.

How many guys do you know who are unhappy or unsuccessful but can attract women? None!

Women are not typically drawn to men who are unsuccessful in life. They are unlikely to be attracted to those who are discontent with their circumstances.

Now, the question arises:

How can you attain happiness and success in life?

Indeed, achieving success and happiness overnight is not easy, but it is not impossible either. It all boils down to shifting your mindset and perspective on life. There are certain factors that can lead to both happiness and success, transforming you into a genuine chick magnet.

Cultivate the Mindset of a Chick Magnet

To embody the charisma of a magnet for female attention, it is essential to immerse yourself in a mindset that exudes confidence, charm, and positivity. These guidelines offer a roadmap to cultivate an irresistible aura that captivates women's interest and admiration.

Generosity forms the cornerstone of your approach. Women are naturally drawn to men who are generous, both in material offerings and in the generosity of spirit. Demonstrating a willingness to give without expectation fosters an atmosphere of warmth and goodwill.

Maintaining a highly optimistic outlook is paramount. Positivity is infectious, and women are naturally attracted to individuals who radiate optimism and hope. Embrace life with enthusiasm and resilience, and you will find yourself effortlessly drawing women into your orbit.

Fear of rejection can be a significant obstacle in connecting with women. However, adopting a fearless approach is essential. Embrace the possibility of rejection as a natural part of the process. If rebuffed, gracefully accept it and move forward with confidence, knowing that each interaction is an opportunity for growth and discovery.

Belief in oneself is the bedrock of confidence. Affirming your worth and capabilities mentally is crucial. Cultivate a mindset that firmly believes in your inherent value and potential. Remember, confidence begins with the conviction in your own thoughts and abilities.

A genuine smile is a potent tool in your arsenal. It costs nothing but has the power to light up a room and instantly charm those around you. Wear a smile as your most captivating accessory, and watch as it draws women to you like moths to a flame.

A well-developed sense of humor is irresistible to women. Being able to effortlessly tickle their funny bone demonstrates intelligence, wit, and emotional intelligence. Master the art of witty banter and playful teasing, and you will find yourself effortlessly forging connections with women.

Unwavering faith in yourself and your abilities is non-negotiable. Banish self-doubt and embrace a mindset of unwavering confidence. Believe unequivocally that you are deserving of success in your interactions with women. Confidence is magnetic, and when you exude self-assurance, women will naturally be drawn to your presence.

In essence, adopting the mindset of a chick magnet requires a combination of generosity, optimism, fearlessness, self-belief, humor, and unwavering confidence. By embodying these qualities and approaches, you will find yourself irresistibly attractive to women, effortlessly forging meaningful connections and relationships.

Successfully connecting with women

Successfully connecting with women is a nuanced endeavor that demands a multifaceted approach, rooted in fundamental principles of human interaction. While everyone is unique, there are universal guidelines that can facilitate meaningful connections.

First and foremost, respect and empathy form the cornerstone of any interaction. Treating women with respect entails recognizing their autonomy, emotions, and perspectives. Empathy, in turn, requires an understanding of their experiences and emotions, fostering a deeper connection built on mutual understanding and compassion.

Active listening is another indispensable skill in building connections. By attentively tuning in to both verbal and non-verbal cues, one can demonstrate genuine interest in a woman's thoughts and feelings, creating an environment of openness and trust.

Authenticity is paramount. Being true to oneself not only cultivates a sense of trust but also paves the way for genuine connections. Pretense or attempting to mold oneself into someone else's ideal can only lead to superficial relationships devoid of depth and authenticity.

Effective communication serves as the bridge for understanding and connection. Clear and honest expression, coupled with confidence and integrity, fosters open dialogue and mutual respect. It is crucial to strike a balance between confidence and humility, ensuring that assertiveness does not morph into arrogance.

Seeking common ground in interests and values can strengthen bonds and provide a solid foundation for connection. Shared passions or beliefs create avenues for meaningful conversations and shared experiences, fostering a sense of camaraderie and understanding.

A good sense of humor can be a powerful tool in

forging connections, easing tensions, and making interactions enjoyable. However, it is imperative to be mindful of boundaries and refrain from making offensive or inappropriate jokes that may jeopardize the rapport.

Confidence, when tempered with self-respect and humility, is undeniably attractive. Believing in oneself while acknowledging and respecting the worth of others cultivates an environment of mutual admiration and equality.

Supporting and empowering women in their pursuits is essential for fostering healthy and equitable relationships. Encouraging their ambitions and aspirations, rather than seeking to control or dominate, demonstrates genuine care and respect.

Respecting boundaries and seeking explicit consent are non-negotiable aspects of any interaction. Establishing and honoring boundaries, coupled with obtaining consent in romantic or intimate situations, is vital for building trust and ensuring mutual respect and safety.

Finally, embracing a mindset of continuous learning and growth is crucial. Recognizing that successful connections require ongoing effort and self-improvement allows for the evolution of relationships and the deepening of mutual understanding.

In essence, meaningful connections with women are built upon a foundation of mutual respect, understanding, and genuine interest in each other's well-being. By embracing these principles and approaching interactions with an open mind and willingness to adapt, one can forge authentic and fulfilling relationships.

Recognizing the types of women who are most receptive to male approaches

Understanding the nuances of female receptivity to male approaches can significantly enhance one's social interactions. While recognizing that individuals vary greatly in their responses, certain characteristics often indicate a greater openness to engagement.

Firstly, outgoing, and socially active women tend to be more receptive to male approaches. They thrive on interaction and enjoy engaging with others, making it easier for men to initiate conversations with them. Their comfort in social settings facilitates smooth communication and connection-building.

Confidence and assertiveness are also key traits associated with receptivity. Women who exude self-assurance are more likely to welcome interactions with men, feeling secure in their own skin and open to meeting new people. Their confidence creates an inviting atmosphere, encouraging others to approach them with ease.

Approachability plays a crucial role in signaling receptivity. Women who display warmth, friendliness, and open body language indicate their readiness for social interactions, including male approaches. Their welcoming demeanor invites engagement and fosters a sense of ease in communication.

Furthermore, adventurous, and spontaneous women tend to be more open to male approaches. They embrace excitement and novelty, making them willing participants in conversations and interactions with new acquaintances. Their adventurous spirit creates opportunities for engaging exchanges and shared experiences.

Independence and open-mindedness are also indicative of receptivity. Women who value their autonomy and possess broad-minded perspectives are more likely to welcome male approaches, appreciating diversity and different viewpoints. Their openness to new ideas fosters enriching interactions and meaningful connections.

Contextual factors, such as social settings or events, can significantly influence receptivity. Women who find themselves in environments conducive to social interaction, such as parties or group activities, are generally more open to male approaches. They anticipate and welcome social engagement in such settings, facilitating natural interaction.

Non-verbal cues provide valuable insights into receptivity. Women who make eye contact, smile, and display open body language signal their readiness for social interaction, including approaches from men. These positive cues create a welcoming environment for engaging conversation and connection-building.

Shared interests and activities serve as a common ground for engagement. Women who share similar hobbies, passions, or interests are more likely to be receptive to male approaches, as there is already a basis for connection and conversation. Shared experiences facilitate meaningful interactions and deepen rapport.

Some women actively seek new connections or relationships, indicating a higher receptivity to approaches. This eagerness for social engagement may be evident through online dating profiles, social cues, or verbal expressions of interest. Their openness to meeting new people creates opportunities for genuine connection and interaction.

Lastly, initial responses to casual interactions provide clues about receptivity. Women who respond positively, engage in conversation, and show interest in continuing the interaction are likely more receptive to further approaches. Their enthusiasm fosters a conducive environment for building rapport and connection.

Regardless of perceived receptivity, it is essential to approach interactions with respect, sensitivity, and genuine interest in getting to know the individual. Building rapport and connection requires mutual respect, understanding, and authentic engagement, irrespective of the type of woman being approached. By embodying these principles, individuals can navigate social interactions effectively and foster meaningful connections.

4 USING PSYCHOLOGY TO ATTRACT WOMEN

Attraction is often viewed as a positive emotion that one person feels toward another, manifesting in forms such as admiration, love, friendship, or lust.

Several factors influence attraction between individuals, including similarity, physical attractiveness, proximity, and reciprocity.

While these factors can indeed spark attraction, there exists another method of attracting others: utilizing psychology.

It is widely acknowledged that attracting a woman whom you do not know well can be challenging. However, employing certain psychological principles can effectively capture her attention and draw her towards you, simplifying the process of attraction and seduction. By leveraging these psychological principles, you can significantly reduce the likelihood of rejection when approaching a woman.

Interaction with Women of Different Personalities

A fundamental principle of psychology is understanding what topics to discuss and how to engage with women of varying personalities. Women's personalities can generally be classified into three types:

Kinesthetic Women:

These women prefer to communicate through touch and physical sensations. They believe that the essence of things can be discerned through tactile experience. When interacting with kinesthetic women, emphasize words and topics related to feelings or touch.

Visual Women:

Women in this category are stimulated by visual imagery and mental pictures. To effectively engage with them, focus on visual elements in your conversation. Utilize words like "great sight" or "lovely looking night" to appeal to their visual senses.

Auditory Women:

Women categorized as auditory are primarily influenced by what they hear. When conversing with them, emphasize words related to sound to capture their attention and draw them towards you. In essence, aim to stimulate their minds by concentrating on auditory elements during your conversation.

Now that you understand the various personalities of women, how can you determine the personality of a specific woman?

Identifying someone's personality is not as challenging as it may seem. Engage them in conversation about any topic that requires description. As they speak, pay close attention to their choice of words. Notice the recurring words and phrases each woman tends to use. By doing this, you can discern the unique personality traits of each woman and adjust your communication style accordingly.

When you converse with a woman in a manner that aligns with her preferences, you will notice her becoming more open to you. It will not be long before she starts to feel drawn to you. This rapid attraction occurs because, subconsciously, she begins to envision you as her soulmate. As she perceives you in this light, you cease to be a stranger to her. She will feel as though she is known you all her life and that you can understand her completely.

Some men tend to make mistakes when attempting to attract and seduce women.

Common mistakes most men make

Let us examine some of the mistakes that many men often make, along with what you can do to avoid them:

Trying to be an excessively nice guy:

Some men attempt to portray themselves as extremely

nice in hopes of attracting women, but this approach often fails. Women are not typically drawn to men simply because they are nice; instead, they may perceive excessive niceness as neediness. It is important to remember that being overly nice does not create strong physical attraction, nor does it guarantee a woman will fall for you.

Trying to convince a woman to like you:

If a woman is not interested in you, attempting to persuade her to change her feelings is futile. No matter what you say or do, you cannot force someone to be attracted to you. It is essential to accept her decision and move on without investing further time and effort. Once a woman has rejected you, trying to change her mind is unlikely to succeed.

Waiting for her permission or approval:

To persuade and charm women, many men await the women's approval or permission before taking certain actions. They believe that by conforming to the women's desires, they can win their affection. However, this mindset is misguided and can be off-putting to women. Constantly seeking permission or approval can irritate and repel them. Instead, it is important to be confident and assertive without constantly seeking validation.

Affections cannot be purchased:

If you believe that you can win a woman's affection by treating her to expensive dinners or showering her with lavish gifts, you are mistaken. She may reject you in favor of someone who treats her with genuine care and attention. Rather than attempting to buy her affection, focus on demonstrating your affection through meaningful actions and thoughtful gestures. Creative expressions of affection are more meaningful than material gifts.

Expressing your feelings after one or two dates:

If you profess your feelings to a woman after only one or two dates, you may scare her away. While this approach may have been effective in the past, it is generally not well-received in modern times. Women may perceive it as a sign that you are primarily interested in physical intimacy rather than building a genuine connection. It is advisable to refrain from expressing strong feelings too early in a relationship and instead focus on getting to know each other gradually.

Believing that women only fall for looks:

If you believed that appearing cool and handsome was enough to make women fall for you, you could not have been more mistaken. Studies have shown that women are attracted to men for more than just their physical appearance. Various other factors, such as communication style and behavior, play significant roles in the attraction process. By leveraging these elements, you can enhance your sexual attractiveness to women.

Believing that money can buy her:

It is a common misconception for men to assume that women are solely interested in money. While there certainly are individuals who prioritize financial wealth, it is unreasonable to generalize that all women are motivated solely by money. Typically, a woman values a man's personality more than his financial status.

Unaware of what to do in different circumstances:

If you are constantly feeling nervous and uncertain about how to act in various situations when you are with a woman, you risk losing her interest. Firstly, it is crucial to recognize that women are perceptive and can often discern your thoughts and feelings. They excel at interpreting body language. Therefore, it is imperative to strategize the steps needed to attract and engage her. Demonstrating your ability to take control of any situation will show her that you possess confidence and competence.

Building emotional connection

This serves as the cornerstone of meaningful relationships, fostering a profound sense of intimacy, trust, and understanding between individuals. It transcends mere surface interactions, delving into the depths of shared experiences and emotions. Let us embark on an exploration of the intricate nuances involved in nurturing and sustaining emotional connection:

Authenticity and vulnerability lie at the heart of genuine emotional connection. It demands individuals to bravely unveil their true selves, encompassing their deepest fears, aspirations, and dreams. By creating a haven for mutual understanding and acceptance, authenticity fosters a profound bond between individuals.

The journey of building emotional connection begins with active listening and empathy. It necessitates individuals to attentively tune into the thoughts and emotions of others, seeking to comprehend their perspective and empathizing with their feelings without casting judgment. This empathetic exchange lays the groundwork for a meaningful connection to flourish.

Shared experiences and cherished memories serve as the scaffolding upon which emotional connection is built. Whether embarking on adventures together, sharing moments of laughter, or creating lasting memories, these shared encounters forge an unbreakable bond, fostering a profound sense of closeness and unity.

Transparent communication acts as the lifeblood of emotional connection. It entails fearlessly expressing thoughts, emotions, and concerns while actively listening to and validating the experiences of the other person. Through honest and open dialogue, trust is cultivated, and the emotional bond between individuals is fortified.

Emotional connection thrives in an environment of mutual support and encouragement. Being a steadfast source of support during both the highs and lows of life, offering words of encouragement, and celebrating each other's victories strengthens the emotional connection, solidifying the bond between individuals.

Physical touch and affection play an indispensable role in nurturing emotional connection. From tender embraces to gentle gestures of affection, physical closeness releases oxytocin, the hormone of love, fostering feelings of warmth and intimacy that deepen the emotional bond between individuals.

Shared values and aspirations serve as guiding lights in fostering emotional connection. When individuals align on core beliefs, dreams, and ambitions, they feel deeply understood and supported, thereby strengthening the emotional bond, and cultivating a deeper connection between them.

Respect and appreciation serve as the pillars upon which emotional connection stands. Acknowledging and valuing each other's strengths, contributions, and individuality fosters mutual respect and admiration, deepening the emotional bond and creating a foundation of trust and gratitude.

Investing quality time together is paramount for nurturing emotional connection. Whether engaging in heartfelt conversations, pursuing shared interests, or simply basking in each other's presence, dedicating time to nurture the relationship fosters intimacy and reinforces the connection between individuals.

Consistency and unwavering commitment are essential for sustaining emotional connection over time. By consistently showing up for each other, prioritizing the relationship, and investing time and effort into nurturing the emotional bond, individuals demonstrate their dedication to building a lasting and meaningful connection.

In essence, creating emotional connection involves cultivating authenticity, empathy, and vulnerability, fostering shared experiences and memories, and nurturing open communication and mutual support. By prioritizing these foundational elements, individuals can deepen their bond, strengthen their connection, and cultivate a relationship imbued with trust, understanding, and enduring love.

5 RULES OF REAL-WORLD SEDUCTION

Despite our modern advancements, it remains a common trend for men to initiate contact with women rather than the other way around.

While dating norms and societal expectations have evolved, modern women still appreciate being pursued. To excel in the art of seduction, one must engage in captivating romantic conversations, possess a strong command of language, exude confidence, and master the art of flirting.

When interacting with a woman, understanding her personality provides insight into the appropriate pace to pursue her. It is crucial to maintain focus on the woman you are engaging with and pay attention to her body language, as it often reveals her level of interest.

First encounters with a woman you are attracted to can lead to three scenarios:

When it comes to encountering a woman, you are attracted to, the initial moments can set the stage for various scenarios, each presenting unique opportunities and challenges in the realm of attraction and seduction.

1. Limited Time for Attraction and Seduction

Picture finding yourself in a bustling coffee shop, catching sight of an alluring woman amidst the hurried patrons. In such fleeting encounters, time is of the essence, demanding swift and decisive action. To pique her interest within this brief window, it is crucial to establish rapport swiftly and convey an aura of trustworthiness. Women, naturally cautious, are disinclined to engage with strangers they do not perceive as trustworthy. Therefore, your demeanor should exude authenticity and genuineness. Rapid gestures, such as suggesting a spontaneous coffee date or swiftly exchanging contact information, become pivotal in seizing this ephemeral opportunity for connection.

2. Several Hours Available for Attraction and Seduction

In scenarios where a few hours are at your disposal to engage with the woman, there's ample opportunity to delve deeper into the seduction process. Imagine finding yourself seated next to her on a long-haul flight or sharing a compartment on a train journey. With more time on your side, it becomes essential to employ effective communication skills and masterful body language to captivate her attention and foster a sense of intrigue. Engaging her in meaningful conversation, sharing anecdotes, and subtly flirting can gradually steer the interaction towards a more intimate level, paving the way for potential future encounters.

3. Days or Weeks to Attract and Seduce

In situations affording more extended timeframes, such as chance encounters with a woman at a bookstore or through mutual acquaintances, the seduction process unfolds at a more leisurely pace. Here, the key lies in patience and strategic wooing over a series of interactions. Take advantage of the opportunity to gradually build a connection and deepen your understanding of each other's interests and desires. Engage in stimulating conversations, share experiences, and express genuine interest in her passions. By nurturing the budding connection over days or weeks, you create a foundation for a more meaningful and lasting bond, allowing attraction to blossom organically.

In essence, regardless of the duration of the encounter, each scenario offers its own set of possibilities for attraction and seduction. By adapting your approach to the time available and leveraging your interpersonal skills effectively, you can maximize the potential for creating meaningful connections and fostering romantic intrigue with the woman you desire.

Understanding the stages of seduction:

To truly grasp the intricacies of seduction, one must delve into the nuanced stages that comprise this captivating dance of attraction and desire. Each stage represents a crucial milestone in the journey towards forging a deep and meaningful connection between individuals, paving the way for romantic exploration and intimacy. Let us embark on a comprehensive exploration of the stages of seduction:

Stage 1: Breaking the Ice

The journey of seduction begins with breaking the ice—a delicate dance of initiating casual conversation and fostering mutual understanding. This initial stage sets the foundation for the interaction, allowing individuals to establish a rapport and feel at ease in each other's presence. It is a moment of shared laughter, subtle glances, and genuine curiosity, as both parties navigate the uncharted waters of first impressions.

Stage 2: Building Trust and Connection

As the conversation flows and barriers begin to dissolve, the next stage unfolds—building trust and deepening the connection. Through genuine interaction and meaningful dialogue, individuals peel back the layers of superficiality, revealing glimpses of their authentic selves. It is a process of vulnerability and openness, as trust gradually blossoms like a delicate flower in the fertile soil of mutual understanding.

Stage 3: Cultivating Romantic Feelings

With trust firmly established, the stage is set for the cultivation of romantic feelings between individuals. Sparks of attraction ignite, fueled by shared interests, common values, and a growing sense of emotional resonance. It is a time of heightened anticipation and burgeoning desire, as hearts flutter with the intoxicating thrill of newfound affection.

Stage 4: Initiating Physical Intimacy

As the flames of passion intensify, the inevitable moment arrives—the initiation of physical intimacy. Whether through a gentle touch, a lingering glance, or a tender kiss, individuals bridge the gap between emotional connection and physical closeness. It is a pivotal juncture in the journey of seduction, marking the transition from platonic affection to romantic entanglement.

Stage 5: Strengthening the Bond

With the first sparks of physical intimacy ignited, the final stage unfolds—strengthening the bond between individuals. This involves arranging future dates, exchanging contact information, and solidifying the connection forged through the stages of seduction. It is a time of anticipation and excitement, as both parties eagerly anticipate the next chapter in their burgeoning romance.

In essence, the stages of seduction represent a transformative journey of connection and exploration, guiding individuals through the intricate dance of attraction and desire. From breaking the ice to strengthening the bond, each stage is imbued with its own unique challenges and rewards, ultimately culminating in the creation of deep and meaningful connections that transcend the boundaries of ordinary experience.

Seduce through Conversation:

Engaging in conversation with a woman can lead you down various paths. If your aim is to seduce her, having an effective pick-up line acts as the key to unlock the door. Pick-up lines, jokes, anecdotes, and other conversational elements should be crafted in a manner that allows you to captivate the woman of your choice. The "opener," as it is often called, serves as your initial interaction with the woman, setting the tone for seduction and intimacy to follow.

It is important to recognize that the same opener may not yield the desired results in every situation. While some openers prove universally effective, adjustments may be necessary to tailor the approach to specific contexts. Employing psychological insights to gauge the mood and receptiveness of women is crucial, allowing you to adapt and anticipate their responses.

In essence, the opener should be compelling enough to instantly capture the woman's interest and stimulate her desire to engage with you. This approach can be directed at a single woman or addressed to a group, with the aim of sparking lively discussions and drawing attention.

If you are drawn to a particular woman, directing the opener specifically towards her can pique the interest of others as well. As conversation ensues, pay attention to signs that the women are interested in you, as their focus reflects their thoughts. Gradually, as interaction deepens, some women may be more forthcoming in their engagement while others may remain reserved. However, there is invariably one woman who captures your attention above all others - the one you are eager to seduce.

Transitioning from a stranger to someone capable of engaging successfully with women involves flirting. Light physical contact, such as a gentle brush, can gauge mutual interest and reciprocity. Gradually steering the conversation towards more intimate topics fosters trust and deepens the connection. Once attraction is established and trust is earned, broaching the subject of further intimacy becomes natural, ensuring mutual desire and consent.

Four Most Effective Flirting Techniques:

When it comes to mastering the art of flirting, men often seek techniques that are not only effective but also genuine and respectful. Here, we delve into four of the most impactful flirting techniques, each designed to captivate the attention of women while maintaining authenticity and integrity.

1. Observing Non-Verbal Cues:

A crucial aspect of successful flirting lies in decoding non-verbal cues, which serve as subtle indicators of a woman's interest and receptiveness. Paying close attention to her body language, such as prolonged eye contact, leaning in during conversation, or playful touches, can provide valuable insights into her level of attraction. These cues convey a woman's availability and openness to interaction, allowing you to gauge the situation and respond accordingly. By attuning yourself to these signals, you can initiate flirtatious exchanges with confidence, knowing that your advances are likely to be well-received.

2. Cultivating a Positive Mindset:

Confidence is undeniably attractive, and it emanates from within. Approaching interactions with a positive mindset not only elevates your own mood but also enhances your allure to others. When you exude self-assurance and happiness, it radiates outward, drawing others towards you like a magnet. Embrace optimism and self-assuredness as you navigate social encounters, projecting an aura of confidence that is both irresistible and contagious. By embracing positivity, you create an inviting atmosphere that encourages genuine connections to flourish.

3. Showcasing Individuality and Intrigue:

In a sea of uniformity, standing out from the crowd is essential to capturing a woman's attention. Embrace your unique qualities and interests, infusing them into your appearance, conversation, and demeanor. Whether it's through distinctive clothing choices, captivating hobbies, or engaging anecdotes, showcasing your individuality sets you apart and piques a woman's curiosity. By adding elements of intrigue and allure to your persona, you create an irresistible allure that sparks fascination and intrigue, drawing women into your orbit with effortless charm.

4. Responding to Rejection with Grace:

In the realm of flirting, rejection is an inevitable reality. How you handle rejection speaks volumes about your character and integrity. Even in the face of disappointment, maintain an unwavering sense of politeness and respect. Accept rejection gracefully, acknowledging the other person's decision with dignity and understanding. By demonstrating maturity and grace in the face of rejection, you leave a lasting impression of your character, earning admiration and respect in the process. Moreover, maintaining a positive and respectful demeanor, even in moments of rejection, preserves the possibility of future interactions and ensures that bridges remain unburned.

In essence, the most effective flirting techniques for men blend astute observation, genuine positivity, individuality, and graceful resilience. By honing these skills and embodying these qualities, you can navigate social interactions with confidence, charm, and authenticity, fostering meaningful connections and romantic possibilities along the way.

Approach Women Without Fear of Rejection:

Are you struggling to attract and seduce the hot women you encounter?

If so, pay close attention to what I am about to share with you...

If you are aiming to improve your success with women, there is one crucial skill you need to master: approaching women without any fear of rejection.

It may sound simple, but many men face significant challenges in this aspect of their dating lives. Fear of rejection holds them back from approaching attractive women, as they worry about potential negative outcomes. They become nervous at the thought of possible rejection and struggle to initiate conversations.

However, it is entirely possible to attract and seduce beautiful women. The key lies in overcoming your fear of rejection. By confidently approaching women without fear, you instantly become an attractive individual with a seductive aura.

Allow me to illustrate with an example...

One of my close friends enjoys success in attracting and seducing numerous beautiful women because he harbors almost no fear of rejection. While he acknowledges the possibility of rejection, he does not let negative thoughts consume him. Instead, he focuses on his approach and engages women in conversation.

As demonstrated, individuals free from the fear of rejection tend to achieve greater success with women. Therefore, cultivating this mindset can significantly enhance your interactions with women.

All it takes is learning to exude confidence in every interaction with women. When conversing with women, concentrate on the discussion and strive to eliminate negative thoughts. Relax and enjoy the interaction.

If you feel intimidated by women, it is essential to work on building your confidence and becoming comfortable with approaching attractive women. When you encounter an attractive woman, make a point to approach her without hesitation.

With practice, your nervousness and fears will gradually dissipate as you become accustomed to approaching women. Establishing a routine of approaching and initiating conversations with women will lead to a notable increase in your success. Even if you only occasionally succeed in attracting a woman, you will gain valuable experience in refining your approach techniques and moving closer to overcoming your fear of rejection.

Attracting and seducing hot women is entirely achievable. However, allowing fears and nervousness to hinder you will diminish your chances of success. By honing your approach techniques and boosting your confidence, you will master the art of attraction.

6 HARNESS THE POWER OF HUMOR

Research has revealed that women consider a sense of humor to be one of the most attractive qualities in men. Indeed, everyone enjoys the company of someone with a great sense of humor. It is safe to say that every woman looks for this trait in men, and making a woman laugh can be a potent tool.

If you are interested in seducing a woman, showcasing a good sense of humor is paramount. Making her laugh ensures she has a fantastic time in your presence. Conversely, appearing overly serious can make her uncomfortable. Engaging in light and humorous conversations is key to putting her at ease.

When meeting a woman for the first time, there is typically some initial reservation between both parties due to the lack of familiarity. A sense of humor serves as the essential icebreaker in such situations.

It is evident that individuals who effortlessly evoke laughter tend to attract more women. Their ability to make others laugh draws women towards them naturally. If a woman must choose between a man who brings joy and one who remains solemn, the choice is clear – she will opt for the man who can make her laugh.

Moreover, women are often drawn to men with sharp

intellects. It is well-established that comedians often possess high levels of intelligence. Therefore, when a woman is in the company of a witty man, she perceives him as intelligent, which adds to his appeal. This is not to suggest that one must be a professional comedian to demonstrate intelligence; simply displaying a sense of humor can convey intelligence positively.

Observing friends who possess a knack for humor sheds light on why women are drawn to them. Their ability to make women laugh and enjoy themselves contributes to fulfilling relationships and enjoyable experiences.

What do you believe ultimately captures a woman's interest?

Ultimately, she seeks a man who can consistently bring a smile to her face. It is crucial to recognize that your chances of fostering a deeper connection, even leading to intimacy, increase significantly if you can evoke laughter and alleviate the stresses of her daily life.

However, it is a known fact that not everyone is inherently gifted with a great sense of humor. So, what do these individuals do to attract and seduce women? Does this mean they are doomed to lack a fulfilling sex life? Absolutely not. If you are among these individuals, understand that you too can enjoy a satisfying sex life. The key is to learn how to cultivate a good sense of humor, and the first step is seizing every opportunity to make her laugh. It is not about constantly cracking jokes; rather, it is about capitalizing on moments where humor can naturally arise.

For instance, imagine you are on a date at a coffee shop, and you notice an exceptionally overweight woman nearby. You might jokingly whisper to your date, "Looks like she's on a seriously healthy diet." Of course, I am not suggesting you speak loudly; it is all about sharing a light moment with your date.

Demonstrating a great sense of humor can often lead to invitations to your date's home when you drop her off.

Developing a strong sense of humor takes time and practice, and there will be occasions where seriousness is necessary. Always be mindful that attempting to inject humor where it is inappropriate may risk alienating the woman.

What one woman finds amusing may not resonate with others. So, if a joke falls flat, do not be discouraged; try another approach. You never know, your next joke might be a hit.

Additionally, it is crucial to tread carefully when it comes to teasing women about their appearances. While some may brush it off with laughter, many women are sensitive about their looks due to underlying self-confidence issues. Teasing them about their appearance, even in jest, may lead to offense rather than laughter.

While many single men believe they possess an excellent sense of humor, the reality often differs. Some individuals lack self-awareness regarding their comedic abilities.

Seduction experts often highlight humor as a significant element in the seduction process, yet they may not delve into how to find humor in everyday situations. However, rest assured that effectively utilizing humor can significantly enhance your interactions with women and naturally enhance your sexual attractiveness, as women find humorous men irresistible.

Undoubtedly, mastering the art of seduction can greatly benefit from a well-developed sense of humor.

Ten easy ways to be funny

Chill out:

Okay, the first thing you need to do is relax. You just want to add some spice to your life and conversations, and appear more easygoing. So do not put so much pressure on yourself -- you just want to get people to laugh, or at least smile.

Do not take things seriously:

Ease up on life and yourself; get used to taking things with a grain of salt. See the humor in situations; you will see that most situations, even getting a $200 dollar speeding ticket or falling on a banana peel have humor written all over them -- the trick is finding them and being able to laugh at yourself.

Be pop culture savvy:

You cannot be funny if you do not have any references or material. The broader your general knowledge is, the funnier the remarks you will make. So, the more you know film, TV, music, and everything pop culture, the greater the chance of being funny. Broaden your horizons and stay up-to-date with current events in the news, and you will be surprised at how much material will randomly come to you.

Do not imitate others:

You want to know about famous actors and comedians, but by the same token, you do not want to get caught using someone else's material. So rather than reciting that great Chris Rock line you heard the other night and passing it off as your own, use the joke in Chris Rock's intonation. That way, people know you are using his joke, and it can still be considered hysterical.

Find your style:

Another reason to avoid imitating actors and comedians is because it may not suit your style. You can always take bits and pieces of others' humor, but you will want to adapt your shtick to your own style and personality -- in turn, this will be easier for you and sound more genuine as you will not have to try as hard.

Have a joke pool:

You never know when a situation calls for a joke, like if you are at a lame party, chatting with some acquaintances. This is where a reserve of jokes can come in handy. One-liners and witty comments are the best to have, as they can be used in many contexts. Know your audience:

There is a time and a place for everything, and just like you need to know your audience when giving a speech, you need to know whom you are delivering a joke to. This said, save the dirty jokes for your friends, and the witty comments for your girlfriend's parents.

Get your delivery and timing right:

Being funny is not only about telling great jokes; it is

all in your mannerism, attitude, how you project yourself, and your delivery. Be animated and alive when you speak, and you can make any story funny.

Make eye contact with people, speak with confidence, and everyone will want to hear your stories. On the other hand, if your humor is more dark, sarcastic, or neurotic (a la Woody Allen, Steven Wright, and George Costanza), then play the part and talk in a monotonous voice. Your delivery must go with your humor, and if your timing is off, then it can ruin the entire joke.

Use people as props:

You are not Carrot Top so drop the props. Rather than using objects as props, use people (I did not say to use people as the butt of your jokes). What always gets a rise out of the ladies is trying to sell things to strangers on the street, like selling your wallet to an old lady. Or start talking to your invisible friend -- just make sure others know you are kidding around and have not gone crazy.

Do not worry about bombing:

Your goal is not to strike a 10 on the Laugh-o-Meter, and every great comedian bombs every now and then. So do not worry if no one gets your joke -- just ignore it or laugh at yourself, and whatever you do: do not delve into your bag of jokes and continue trying to make everyone laugh -- you do not want to try too hard.

Final tips:

Smiling is infectious, so if you smile a lot while talking, it will encourage others to laugh. Be animated and energetic when you are telling a story, it will make your stories more interesting and captivate listeners. Be blunt; this usually takes people by surprise and can end up being funny. Make sure your timing is right. When telling a joke, do not laugh before the punch line. Be creative. It will inspire you to be funny.

Remember, you do not need to be the life of the party; being funny is just a great asset in seduction as it makes you look easygoing and approachable, helps you handle certain awkward situations, makes you more sociable, and is a great turn-on to women.

But while you want to be funny, you do not want to be the office clown. If you are typecast as the joker no woman will ever take you seriously, so know when to be funny and when to be serious, or the joke will be on you.

7 MAKE HER CHASE YOU

Okay, so there is a woman whom you really like, and you would love to sleep with her. Check out the tips given below which can help you to seduce her:

Do not consider yourself as unattractive - If you feel that you are not attractive, then there is no way in which you can make the woman find you attractive. This type of thinking will influence your body language and the way you think. So, start telling yourself that you are attractive.

Do not bore her - There are times when men tend to bore women without even realizing that they are doing that. Never talk about your work, sports, or weather when you are with a lady.

Do not talk too much - Talking a lot can make the lady turn her back on you. She will know that you are babbling because of nervousness. Try to keep the conversation moderate.

Never ask too many questions - I know it is weird when you are with a woman and have nothing to talk about. However, this does not mean that you must keep asking her questions after questions. Asking a few questions can make a conversation interesting but asking too many questions will make the lady want to run away from you.

Do not treat a woman as a prize - A woman does not like the idea of her being a prize. She will not be attracted to you if you think that you must win the 'prize.'

Try to interpret her body language - Many men do not understand that it is necessary to read the body language of the women that they are interested in. By reading her body language you will have some idea about whether she is keen on you. If she is then you can carry out your seduction plan, and if she is not there are a lot of other fishes in the sea.

Flirting is the answer - How will a woman know that you are interested in her if you do not give her a sign? When you flirt with her, you indirectly let her know about your intention.

Be confident - Women simply cannot resist men who are confident. Do not be afraid to approach a woman because of fear of rejection. There are always risks in life, and if you do not take the risk then you cannot reap the benefits.

Make the lady feel good - If you want to attract and seduce a lady, it is very important to make her feel good in your company. If she feels pleasant in your company then it will not take a long time to attract her towards you and then take one more step towards seducing her.

Have a good sense of humor - Women love those men who can make them laugh. If you have a good sense of humor then there are more chances of your attracting and seducing the lady that you like.

Create Mystery by Sending Mixed Signals

If you think being steady and uniform in your behavior, will keep your woman happy, think again. By being unvarying and regular, you are merely telling her how good a boring you might be! Now that is an incorrect approach, during your dating days, because you are truly giving the wrong signal at the wrong time. To invoke intensity and fervor in your relationship, the secret lies in being unpredictable. Never let the cat out of the bag, as to your true intentions. Because normal is boring, in dating terms.

Here are some purposeful confusing signals:

Be a wizard with numbers – narrate her cell number beginning backwards! Ensure she knows your numbers too. But surprise! Pretend to have forgotten her contact details, ask for it again.

Act distant and unapproachable on a date. Look through her at times, without being rude or impolite. Pretend your mind is somewhere else.

Women love to be surprised. Appear suddenly at

places and times, when she least expects you. Give a bear hug, kiss her, when she is least prepared, and then move on to do something else completely different.

Compliment her on her dress that day, only to change your opinion later. Basic idea is to appear inconsistent.

Sometimes do things which she least expects you to do. Like going for a kid film together or dining at a restaurant, which she did not even know existed. Outbid her assumptions at every step.

Such conflicting and inconsistent behavioral traits stimulate a woman, and display your erratic and mercurial temperament. But let us not do this too frequently, or she might get the impression that you are some sort of loony that she has landed up with. Act a little mad, but not totally mad. So that you emerge as an otherwise dependable and trustworthy companion.

The secret behind creating magic in any dating relationship is generating a healthy blend of contradictions. Acting close as well as distant, being decisive as well as vacillating, getting romantic and suddenly playing aloof, all goes to create those magical moments, we all yearn for. Playing hide and seek so to speak, will help you not only attract women but keep them consistently attracted. The best example that comes to my mind is a tight-rope walker in a circus arena. He is extremely careful on that rope while walking, neither too fast nor too slow, because either way he falls. If you watch closely, he appears inconsistent while walking, but look closer, there is a method in his madness.

Similarly, if you have tried to walk with a cup of hot coffee brimming up to the edges, you try and adjust your pace, to prevent it from splashing over your arm. You do not walk at a uniform pace; you keep adjusting it all the way till you reach your destination. Your inconsistency in the dating game, acts very much the same way, keeping the cup of passion full, without any spillage, till you reach your determined goal.

How to Intrigue any Woman?

A dull, boring, lackluster, and predictable individual would not interest anybody. This is especially true for all women in general. Women can find more interesting things to do like reading a book or watching the television than having to bear with someone who would bore them to death. The thing about women is that they like surprises and they like excitement, and it is important for them to get away occasionally, from their humdrum existence.

Men who have dull, boring, lackluster, and predictable qualities have the tendency to be shunned by women simply because they do not have enough suspense or excitement in their personalities to be able to generate interest from the opposite sex. Women want men who would be able to tickle their brains and make them think. They want men who would be able to create ways of exciting them even in the simplest way possible.

Boring women is not the issue. Intriguing women is. Intriguing women and getting their attention is something that has worked for most men over the years, because men who know how to intrigue women cause women themselves to constantly wonder about what they are thinking of or what they are going to do next. It is intrigue which keeps them fascinating in the eyes of women who have close encounters with them one way or another.

Intriguing women is not an easy task. Intriguing women means fascinating them by varying one's presentation of himself. Doing this would make the man concerned unpredictable in every way. To be able to intrigue women, it is advisable for men who like to dress in coat and tie to dress down occasionally. Intriguing women would mean that guys who like to have the same haircut would have to start considering sporting new hairdos that would alter their looks dramatically. Those who like to indulge in the same things repeatedly should think about trying out something new to be able to intrigue women even more. Those bent on exerting enough effort to intrigue women should always remember that sticking to the same old things and the same old routines would not actually help if one wants to have a personality that exudes thrill and unpredictability.

To be able to intrigue women, it should be borne in mind that women get excited about the unexpected. This is the reason why it is important for men to stay as unpredictable as they can be. Not knowing what would happen next is something that would come as a pleasant surprise to any woman who has had her part in seeing and experiencing what is outright common and ordinary.

Exercising a little effort on the part of men to be able to intrigue women is something that women would be able to appreciate, because it is the binding force that would make them want to know more about the man concerned apart from what they already do.

Men should remember that to be able to intrigue women, it is always important to have an air of mystery around themselves. This is what will draw women to their feet.

A well-read book is not as interesting as that which is fresh, and it is this novelty which will render it more than exciting as compared to all the rest.

8 GET INTO THE MINDS OF WOMEN

Have you ever wondered what goes inside the minds of women? It is a known fact that men can never understand how the women think. However, there are certain ways in which all the women think and, in this chapter, we are going to learn that.

When a woman sees an extremely attractive man, her first thought would be 'he is so hot.' That is right. Your ears are working extremely well, so believe what I have just said. If you thought that only men could think that way then you do not know a lot. However, seeing a hot and attractive guy does not mean that the woman would approach him. If she is really interested in one guy then you will find that she will continue to look at him and this is a way of letting him know that she wants to be approached. If the guy in question is also interested, then he will probably do the approaching.

So, the next time you find a woman staring at you, approach her because she will not approach you first.

Never let a woman think that you are a 'nice' guy if you are attracted to her. This would mean that she is willing to be your friend but nothing more than a friend. She will go out with you, but you would only be 'useful friend' to her with the help of which she can date other men. However, this does not mean that you must be a bad guy.

The mind of a woman is such that they are attracted to guys whom they find mysterious. If she comes across a guy who looks mystifying then in her mind, she would wonder why he behaves the way he does. This will draw her towards him. Women like to unravel mysteries, and they simply cannot resist the challenge to know more about mysterious men.

If a woman fancies you then you will know it. Like I mentioned earlier, she is attracted to you if she cannot take her eyes off you. However, if you find her eyes wandering somewhere else when she is talking to you then you should know that she is not interested. Find someone else who is interested in you.

Women are very keen creatures who simply love to notice a lot of tiny details. The first thing that she will notice about you is your body language. By checking out your body language, a woman can find out a lot about your personality. For example, if you are nervous then she will know. Women have the tendency to observe the body language ten times more than men do. If you want to impress her then you should know how to act and behave when she is around. Reading some books on body language can be helpful.

The women love men who are full of confidence. If a confident man approaches a woman, then he has more chances to seduce her. To some extent, confidence indicates power and women simply cannot resist powerful men.

How to figure out what she really means?

Women and men communicate differently with women being more verbal and vocal and men not so much. Women are also much more emotional and many would "argue" speak an entirely different language altogether. And many would insist that they encode what they mean or are trying to say behind frivolous words and phrases.

But, if you have got to understand her, it is up to YOU to figure her out and figure out what she really means.

Sorry Situations: Just because she apologizes does not mean she thinks she was wrong (in fact she probably does not believe she was). All it really means is that she is initiating the reconciliation, and the LEAST she expects you to do is admit your faults and say you are sorry too.

Weighty Issues: Most women want and need to be affirmed and want to know that they are still attractive to their man. So, when she asks if she looks fat, she is simply fishing for compliments and wants to know you think of her as beautiful. Make sure your answer is honest BUT accentuates her attractiveness and her appeal (In fact, if you do not like how she looks, you may want to say, you look lovely in that but I tend to prefer you in a dress, or pants, or in that red outfit, etc.)

Her Get Up and Go: She may start hinting that she is tired or has lots to do tomorrow. She may even suggest that you stay behind and have a good time. Dude, that is you cue to get ready to go.

Kidding Around: She may be complimenting you sense of humor and your disposition with nieces and nephews, but she wants to know your thoughts on kids, having some of your own, and how soon. Even if you do not foresee having children in the immediate future, keep in mind that ladies like to look ahead, well ahead, so, if you are not opposed to the idea (even if it is down the road) give her the answer she is fishing for, or come up with an equally indirect response of your own.

Fine And Seek: She gives every indication that there may be something wrong, but when you ask, she assures you it is "nothing". Well guys, you just may be damned if you do and damned if you do not. If you take it at face value that everything is status quo, she will continue being annoyed, but if do your job and identify the problem, you just may be in for a fight. But, remember she's WAITING for you to figure it out and to be given the chance to get it off her chest.

Seduction for Positive Influence

Seduction for Positive Influence embodies the delicate art of persuasion and influence with the noble intention of nurturing beneficial outcomes and fostering genuine relationships. It delves into the realm of interpersonal dynamics, employing charm, charisma, and adept communication to engage and sway others towards mutually beneficial ends. Here, we embark on a comprehensive exploration of how the art of seduction can be harnessed to cultivate positive influence:

At its core, the bedrock of positive influence lies in the establishment of trust and rapport. Seduction within this framework involves the sincere cultivation of connections with individuals, comprehending their needs, and forging relationships grounded in mutual respect and understanding.

Effective seduction for positive influence initiates with the practice of active listening and empathy. By attentively absorbing others' perspectives and empathizing with their emotions, one can forge deeper connections and tailor their approach to resonate with their values and interests.

Central to the art of seduction is charismatic communication. Mastery of this skill encompasses the nuances of body language, tone of voice, and the selection of words, all of which are employed to captivate others and inspire them to embrace new ideas or viewpoints.

Seduction can serve as a catalyst for fostering collaboration and cooperation among individuals or groups. By spotlighting shared goals and accentuating the advantages of collective effort, one can motivate others to unite their strengths and accomplish mutual objectives.

Inspirational leadership is another facet of seduction for positive influence. Leaders who exude charisma possess the ability to inspire and motivate others to unlock their full potential. By leading by example, articulating a compelling vision, and instilling confidence in others, a culture of empowerment and success can be nurtured.

The art of seduction extends its reach into the realm of negotiation and conflict resolution. Through astute comprehension of the interests and motivations of all involved parties, skilled practitioners can adeptly navigate differences and craft solutions that satisfy the needs of all stakeholders.

At its heart, positive influence through seduction revolves around the creation of win-win scenarios. By actively seeking opportunities for collaboration and compromise, one can cultivate relationships founded on reciprocity and mutual benefit, nurturing an environment conducive to growth and success.

Ethical considerations serve as an indispensable guiding principle in the realm of seduction for positive influence. It is imperative that all actions and interactions be conducted with integrity and honesty, devoid of manipulative or deceptive tactics that can erode trust and undermine relationships.

An integral aspect of seduction for positive influence lies in empowering others to make informed decisions and assume ownership of their actions. By offering support, encouragement, and resources, individuals can help others realize their potential and achieve their goals.

Continuous improvement and learning form the cornerstone of mastery in seduction for positive influence. By actively seeking feedback, assimilating insights from experiences, and perpetually refining interpersonal skills, one can evolve into a more adept influencer and catalyst for positive change.

In essence, seduction for positive influence harnesses the power of charm, charisma, and interpersonal finesse to cultivate trust, inspire collaboration, and motivate others to achieve their aspirations. Approaching interactions with authenticity, empathy, and integrity, practitioners of this art leverage its potential to foster meaningful connections and drive positive outcomes across personal and professional domains.

9 THE MYSTERY OF SEDUCTION DEMYSTIFIED

Seduction is a splendor game and it is not difficult to play this game. What you really need in this game is lots of confidence and some tips on social psychology. By ways of conformity and persuasion, you can influence and seduce the person in front of you. It does not matter whether you know the person or not.

Walk into a bar or a lounge and start a conversation with the person that you are attracted to. This may require a lot of confidence initially. Confidence has nothing to do with height, stature or looks. It is an inherent power lying inside of you. If you think that you can do it then it will show. This comes out in your inherent personal communication skills.

The art of seduction lies within a person. You should make use the powers of persuasion. This means that you need to know what turns a person on and what turns a person off. When you know what motivates a person to be drawn towards you, use your persuasive skills to draw the person closer to you. The seduction must be the first step in the foreplay. Many of the old texts talk about sex and how to go about the various positions. However, seduction is more than just sex. It is what sets your partner on fire and make her want to have you more than anything else that she desires.

You should get to know her psychologically. Use your powers of persuasion to get what you want. To begin with you can try thinking of the things which she may have in her mind. Usually, all women will give subtle or even direct hints. Catch those hints and influence her thinking. Within the first few minutes, you can have her eating out of your palms.

Women like men to be in control and feel wanted. This is the reason that even now, some of the smartest and the most beautiful women are not seen alongside the richer and more famous. Some of these rich and famous people do not have time for these gorgeous women, and these women then seek solace elsewhere. Who does not know of Diana, the late princess? If you really want to attract the Diana's of the world, then you must listen to them and pay them attention.

Do not say things that the women would expect you to say. Instead, you should say some of the things that are least likely to be said so that there is always a surprise element in your conversation. Use social psychology to understand how she would react to you. Humans have an inherent ability to interact and react to another person. Since you are different and you make her feel wanted, she would be happy to be seduced by you. All women are looking for relationships where they want to feel loved, cared and protected for. If you can provide this semblance through your communication skills, then you have got what you are looking for.

The 'mystery method' of seduction is not an unheard term for all those who have been looking out for the different techniques to seduce women. So, what is the mystery method of seduction? In a very simple word, this is a step-by-step method which can be learnt.

According to the mystery method, men assess their potential partners by their replication value. On the other hand, women assess their potential partners by their survival value. The mystery method states that individuals have a powerful emotional reaction to individuals with higher value. This is the reason why men have a powerful reaction to extremely attractive women. It is because of this reaction that men undergo an adrenaline rush, and they have the tendency to behave in a 'strange' way when they are around attractive women.

A woman who is extremely attractive would create such a type of reaction in most men. So according to the mystery method the woman would subconsciously find the man, who looks emotionally unresponsive to her, of higher value. As a result, she will be drawn towards him as he poses a challenge for her.

How to use the three elements of seduction?

Basically, there are three elements or components in the mystery method of seduction, and they are as follows:

Attract.

Comfort.

Seduce.

Each of these elements is categorized into three phases.

Let us look at the three phases and all the components of this method:

Attract 1 (A1): In this phase, you need to start a conversation with the woman or induce her to start one. Conversation is very important and you should not take the next step, unless you engage yourself in a good conversation. The A1 stage is extremely significant even though it does not last for a long time. If you see an extremely attractive woman that you like, proceed towards her direction to approach her. It is always recommended that you should not walk to her from the back nor should you walk straight into her direction. You can walk at a 45–90-degree angle. Use dismissive body language to start a conversation. Use short but unique lines to impress her instead of babbling a long story or telling her that you like her dress.

Attract 2 (A2): Many men are of the opinion that getting the women attracted to them is not simple. This is an incorrect thinking because you can attract women very easily. You simply must make use of certain techniques like showing higher social value, confident male traits, etc. Most of the time, this stage takes about two to ten minutes. However, it may take up to twenty minutes with some women. Always remember that you should not praise her on her looks at this stage. When she shows an interest in you, step to the next stage i.e. A3.

Attract 3 (A3): This is a very significant stage. Here you must let the woman know that you are attracted to her not just because of her appearances. If you merely state that you are interested in her simply because she is beautiful then she will turn her back on you. This will happen because the lady will think that you are not as cool as she thought you were. Women will not want to go out with you if they find that you are 'easy.' If you are 'hard to get' then you will find women hovering about you. Talk about her life in general and compliment her and not on her appearances only if the situation asks for it.

Comfort (C1, C2 and C3): Creating a comfortable atmosphere is very important in the seduction process. Majority of the women (except for the party girls) will take a minimum of three to ten hours and perhaps more than one meeting to get in to the comfort phase. C1 or the 'connection' phase will occur in the location where you have first attracted the lady. C2 or the 'trust' stage will take place in a more comfortable location. Lastly, C3 or the 'intimacy' stage will take place in the place where you plan to seduce her.

Seduction (S1, S2 and S3): S1 is the arousal stage where you must turn her on. S2 is the stage of resistance where the woman would resist you as she would not like to think of herself as a 'slut'. In this stage, you need to convince her to change her mind with your seduction technique. In S3 is the stage where you get in to bed with her. Always remember to seduce her in a place where you will not be disturbed.

If you are planning to seduce her in your own home then make sure that your home is clean and hygienic. Many women find the idea of an untidy place abhorring. You may have aroused her, but if she finds that your place is unclean and untidy then she may change her mind. I am not saying that your home should be spotless. Just clean enough to make her comfortable in your home.

There are certain things that you can use to add comfort to the environment such as whipped cream, strawberries, chocolates, and champagne.

Calibration Value

In this section I will expand more the concept of value and calibrating value in a relationship with a female.

The concept of value in a relationship is the same like

the concept of value in the commercial world with the big difference that in the case of an emotional and sexual relationship with a woman it relates to the deeper instincts of evolution and replicating.

For example, in a situation of war the fact that you are a skilled warrior and have big muscles is for sure of very important replicating and evolutionary value for her (it helps her to survive).

Instead, a very ugly, short, and fat guy may have for her - and surely has - a very important evolutionary and replicating value if he has a lot of money if she is planning to make a family and have children.

It is also a very variable concept: if you are in a modern environment your Ferrari surely has a very important value in her eyes for the choice of a mate but it is totally worthless for her if you are in a desert without water and what she values then is getting a chance to satisfy thirsty.

To understand the concept of value in a relationship you need to see it as a process.

What she values now may be totally different than what she values later.

This is for example evident when women remain at home from work in modern "politically correct" countries and get money from the social security.

In that stage of their life, they may very much value a fat, short guy without pick-up and seduction skills who makes decent money instead of the good looking "bad boy" who makes them tickle.

Then when they get back to work after having been 3-4 years at home taking care of the children while he pays the bills they may - either consciously or unconsciously - try to feel that their partner has no value anymore despite all his money and start to feel attraction for the bad boy.

That is perfectly in line with what biology and evolution look for: spreading different genes in as many different directions as possible.

Being boyfriend/girlfriend or being married and exclusive are social constructs. Agreements. Not what Nature's target really is.

So, to keep attraction on in a relationship you must calibrate value.

This is very difficult because a female active tendency to control you is always a direct attempt to lower your value. The purpose of her controlling attempts is to lower your value in a relationship to access your resources and make sure you will be loyal to her along the pregnancy and the first years of the child bearing.

So, to calibrate value in a relationship with a woman you need to counter act her active controlling attempt. At the same time, you need to be careful of not putting her "too much" down otherwise you will cause big problems to her self-esteem.

Examples of calibrating value in a relationship:

She lowers your value by flirting with another guy in front of your eyes.

You shout to her and maybe become violent: that is a mis-calibration. Whatever the outcome is you will put her too much down and the relationship will get bad. Also, you will surely incur into legal problems and maybe get jailed.

Instead, a proper way of reacting to it is to wait a week and show her how you can flirt with another woman in front of her eyes or even use rich descriptions to simply describe verbally - without even really flirting - a situation where you are being liked a lot by other women.

That is fair and proper calibration. You also must promptly stop doing this as soon as she starts to show respect again. Doing it too much would be another mis- calibration.

As a man you are - especially if she is pregnant and having little children - in a position of power. So, you must use that power but not "too much" otherwise you are putting her down and badly mis-calibrating.

She lowers your value by comparing your economic achievements to the economic achievements of other guys.

This is a bad one: there will always be someone richer than you.

Telling her straight to her face that she is a bitch and a prostitute in her nature will only show weakness and put her too much down. Women do these things out of instinct (well some of them in purpose but that is a smaller group).

Instead telling her: "I am sure that one day you will have a lot of money on your bank account" gives her an indirect message of how silly she is being with her manipulation attempt and puts her in her place without putting her too much down.

The use of positive frames is extremely powerful in calibrating value.

For example:

Hot Babe: "I had a wonderful ride on this guy's Ferrari,

he is a very skilled driver.

Johnny: "I am happy for you. I am sure one day you will have your own Ferrari and that wonderful villa in Miami you have been dreaming of."

Then after a week:

Johnny: "By the way: I had a lot of work today. I just hired a couple of new secretaries; one Maria is 18 and just started her career. She looks and acts gorgeous but it will be a hell of a job to train her."

Hot Babe: "Hmm... I hope you do not find her too gorgeous and keep your hands off her."
Johnny: "Are you kidding me baby? It is wonderful for the image of the Company to have new gorgeous secretaries."

See guys? These are some examples of calibrating value in a relationship with a woman.

Put your energy into business, pick-up, and seduction and never enter a relationship where you are being made weaker!

To be able to understand the right way of calibrating value in a relationship with a woman is a very important skill.

If you are a single man willing to seduce women to get a wonderful girlfriend.

Or a husband willing to make his own wife happy in the relationship.
Or a playboy willing to have a lot of fun.

10 SUN SIGNS & PERSONALITY OF WOWEN

I know many people who underestimate the importance of sun signs. There are few men who feel that only women are interested in horoscopes and sun signs. However, I think getting to know more about the sun signs can help you develop your seduction plan. You must be thinking how it can help you.

You see, when you know more about the traits of each sun sign you automatically will have some knowledge about the women. Most of the traits mentioned in the different sun signs are like the traits of women born under those signs. Thus, you can generally figure out about the personality of a woman if you know what her sun sign is.

In addition to this, most women are interested in horoscopes so you can make your conversation more interesting by talking about the traits of different sun signs and compatibility between various sun signs.

Now let us look at the different sun signs and what kind of seduction technique you can use for each sign:

Aries (March 19th to April 18th) - Women born under the sign of Aries prefer their men to be aggressive and bold. If you want to kiss her then do not wait and ask for her approval. Just surprise her by giving her an out-of-the- world and mind-blowing kiss. The approach you take should have some force. In addition, the Aries women love it when men pay compliments to them. In case you have met an Aries woman for the first time then do not feel that you must restrain yourself to disagree with them on certain matters simply because you want to seduce them. Women born under this sign are drawn to men who disagree with them. Those who are born under this sign prefers sweet, positive, and swift style of seduction.

Taurus (April 19th to May 19th) - If you are attracted to a woman who is born under the sign of Taurus then your seduction style should be steady but slow. The women born under this sign relish and cherish wooing stage of a relationship. When you are going on a first date with her then make sure that you do not arrive late. Always arrive before her and buy her some gifts or flowers. These women simply love it when men offer them gifts. If you want to seduce a lady born under this sign then use a subtle spray of cologne as ladies are very much influenced by sensual stimuli. These women also love sense of humor. You can attract a woman towards you with great jokes.

Gemini (May 20th to June 19th) - Women born under this sign have a high level of intelligence. So, the best way to seduce the women born under this sun sign would be to consult them about intellectual matters. These women usually fall for professional experts. You should know that Gemini women love to flirt. In fact, they are good at flirting and there is nothing else they would love to do than flirt with the opposite sex.

Cancer (June 20th to July 21st) - Women born under the sign of Cancer are usually soft at heart. In case you are attracted to a woman who is born under this sun sign then the best way to seduce her and get her into your bed would be to display the sensitive side of your personality to her. One great way to impress her would be to mention your interest in charities, particularly those concerning children. These women love to be taken care of, and if you want to seduce a woman of this sun sign then you can think of cooking dinner for her. These women are very romantic, and they love the romantic surroundings. If you are cooking for her then play a soft music in the background and create a romantic atmosphere by using candles. If you want to kiss her then ask for her permission first otherwise, she may not take it well. Your style of seduction should be nurturing and soft.

Leo (July 22nd to August 21st) - It is very important to concentrate on the women of this sun sign if you want to seduce them. They love it when men praise them on, the way they dress, behave, eat, talk, etc. In short, they love hearing men singing their praises. These women love to have the best, and if you want to make a good impression then treat her the best possible way. If you do that then you will find that these women would be drawn to you and the seduction process would become easy and simple. At the time of foreplay, make sure that you whisper words of compliments in her ears. Doing this would make your lovemaking fabulous and out of the world. The women under this sign have an innate seduction personality. If you can make her fall for you then you can be sure that she would meet you more than half way in the seduction process.

Virgo (August 22nd to September 21st) - If you are thinking of seducing a woman born under the sign of Virgo then cleanliness would most definitely be an asset. If you are taking her to your place then first ensure that your sheets are clean and fresh before you place her on your bed. The most important thing is that you should look smart as well as clean. These women get turned on by seeing clean, hygienic, and clever men. If you fancy a woman of this sign then you should dress properly when you are meeting her. They get aroused by the smell of your cologne. If you want the seduction to be perfect then you can try having a shower together with her. In case you have just met a woman and want to break the ice between the two of you then you can consider asking her for help in finding your mobile phone, proofreading some notes, or even organizing your desk. The reason is that the women of this sun sign like help others.

Libra (September 22nd to October 21st) - Libras are very classy and stylish. If you are interested in seducing a Libran woman then you need to think of romancing her in a very sophisticated manner. These women love beautiful and stylish things. They would expect you to do everything with style. Women born under the sign of Libra love listening to music. So, it would be a great idea to take her to a concert before seducing her. In addition, make sure that you kiss extremely well before you try to seduce a Libran. Libras simply love men who have skills in lovemaking. For Libras, seduction is an inborn talent. They have innate seduction skills, and they also expect you to seduce them in the best possible way that would make them screaming for more.

Scorpio (October 22nd to November 20th) - Most men find it a bit difficult to seduce scorpions because these women are full of secrets, and you never know what you can expect from them. You should not be put off if she gives you a 'difficult to understand' smile when you make a move on her. Her ways of showing attraction towards you are inscrutable most of the time. If you want to seduce her then take her out for a film and play with her hands during the movie. This will arouse her and make your lovemaking impeccable later. At the time of making love, your moves should be urgent and yet the lovemaking should be without any words. Allow your body to do all the talking. Simply indulge in her and give her the best seduction that one can offer.

Sagittarius (November 21st to December 20th) - If you have a great sense of humor than you can very easily seduce and have a Sagittarian woman in your bed. Women born under this sign simply love men who can make them laugh all the time. If you want to get a Sagittarian woman to bed then you can attract her towards you by telling her jokes and being humorous. These women love the idea to great sex in the outdoors. One great idea to seduce her would be to take her out for camping. Remember to take a double sleeping bag with you. These women have mischievous and naughty methods of seduction themselves, and if you can make her fall for you then you are in for a great roll in the sack.

Capricorn (December 21st to January 18th) - These are noble women but do not worry because seducing a woman born under this sun sign would be worth all the efforts. If you want to seduce them then you should not hurry. Be patient and use a slow but steady approach when you are seducing her. When you are out on a first date, do not try to have more than a long-lasting kiss. Now on your next date, you can caress her neck, shoulders or back. Remember to make use of firm and persistent pressure when you are caressing her. This will turn her on, and she will ask you to continue what you started. At this time, try to pull back a little because a woman born under this are of the opinion that a person should wait for the best to happen. When you pull back, tell her that it would be better if you two waits for some time before moving on to the next level. Doing this will impress her tremendously, and it will make your seduction more exciting.

Aquarius (January 21st to February 18th) - On the sexual front, you will discover that it is not very easy to seduce an Aquarian woman. You should make use or think of a unique approach if you want to seduce her. The Aquarian women love original things and in the matter of seduction, they would also expect something original. Always remember that the more unusual you act and behave, the more you will be able to get her attracted towards you. Most of the women born under this sign simply cannot resist the challenge. You can even challenge her to kiss or go out on a date with you.

Pisces (February 18th to March 18th) - Are you attracted to a Piscean woman? If this is the case then you will have to make her feel out of the world if you want to seduce her. One good idea would be to invite the lady to your home to show her your aquarium. You should start your seduction process when she is engrossed in seeing fishes in your aquarium. Give her a kiss on the shoulders and this will automatically lead her to your bedroom. You can increase the attraction and make the seduction much better by massaging her feet. They are very sensitive and have a soft heart so try to seduce her slowly but skillfully.

It is a known fact that one can find out more about another person, without asking any questions by reading the traits of the sun sign, which the lady you like is born under. By reading this, I am sure you will have some idea about how to behave, and what you expect when you are with women belonging to different star signs.

11 BREAKING SEDUCTION MYTHS & BUILDING CONFIDENCE

Whether we admit it or not but seduction is not something which every man is capable of. Some are experts in seducing women, whereas some men are not bothered to learn the art of seduction.

Seduction is not at all difficult if you have proper knowledge in this subject. In this chapter, we are going to look at some of the myths of seduction.

Rejection means I cannot seduce any woman - Many men who have been rejected by women are of the opinion that they will not be able to approach and seduce other women. This is simply a myth and believe me, there are many men who have got rejected, but they also could seduce the women they liked in some later stage. Just because you got rejected by one woman does not mean that every woman will reject you. Maybe that woman who rejected you was not attracted to you. This is a common scenario, and you should get over it. Always remember that every single man has been rejected in his life at least once. Why should you allow one rejection to have a negative impact on your sex life?

I cannot seduce any one - If you think that you do not have it in you to seduce a woman then you could not be more wrong. Each of us has been born with innate seduction techniques. You may not have discovered it yet but this does not mean that you cannot seduce a woman. How will you know that seduction is not for you if you do not try it? Have more confidence in yourself. Try seducing a woman that you are attracted to. If she is interested in you then you can easily seduce her, and if she is not interested then move over to another woman.

Women would think that I am a jerk - This is simply not true. Both men as well as women have a sex life, and they will not think that you are a jerk if you try to attract her. How do you think a man and a woman get in to a relationship? The man must have approached the woman first. If the woman you like is not interested then she will politely tell you that she is with someone. If she appears to be offended then you should steer away from her. On the other hand, if she laughs at you then something is terribly wrong with her.

The woman will not choose me - Now this signifies lack of confidence in yourself. There are so many men who approach women without having this kind of thought. Nothing is wrong with you so there is no reason why she would not go for you. If you want to seduce a woman then you should first have faith in yourself. Women are attracted to men who are confident and there is no way a woman would go for you if you lack self-confidence. Build up your self-confidence at first before approaching any woman.

You will be able to seduce a woman if only you convince yourself that you can seduce her. Negative thinking will not help you with seduction.

It is important to sing her praises to seduce her - This is just not true. Some women like men who complement them, but they are not obsessed, with compliments. Believe it or not but there are few women who would feel insulted when you praise her body, dress, or physical appearance. There are women who do not care about compliments because they feel that men simply compliment them to get in to their pants. So, the next time you are with a woman that you want to seduce, try not to sing too many praises for you may push her away from you.

It is important for me to be extremely creative and funny- This is not important. When you are not creative, a woman will be able to tell. She is extremely good at reading body languages. Do not force yourself to look creative or funny if you are not. There is a possibility of your ending up looking extremely stupid. Just relax. If you are not comfortable with cracking jokes then you do not have to do that. Instead, you can do or talk about something that you are good at.

By reading all the methods of seduction, I will be an excellent seducer - This is a false believe. Sure, reading about the methods of seduction will help you, but you may not be able to master it if you do not try to understand and practice the methods. Moreover, you cannot be an expert in seduction in one or two days. It may take a few weeks or months for you to master it.

Women love money - This may hold true for some women but not all women are after you for your money. If there is no attraction then there is no way in, which you can successfully seduce a woman, no matter how rich or wealthy you are.

12 RELATIONSHIP SECRETS

This chapter is included to give your insight into how you can create a relationship after you have managed to seduce a woman. Most men really have very little understanding of how women view relationships. So even after the initial success they often fail to sustain those gains. So read on and enlighten your knowledge.

How to Bond with Your Partner?

Many partners attempt to bond with candles, wine, or lingerie, only to find their time together feeling flat, empty, and passionless. In this section, discover what really creates bonding, intimacy, and passion with your partner.

Bonding has nothing to do with candles, wine, and expensive lingerie. It has to do with INTENT. In any given moment we are in one of two possible intents:

- The intent to have control over getting love and avoiding pain.
- The intent to learn about being loving to ourselves and to others.

Virtually all of us have learned many ways of trying to have control over getting love and avoiding pain. We learned these protective behaviors when we were children, and as adults we unconsciously continue these learned controlling behaviors, such as anger, criticism, withdrawal, resistance, or compliance. For most people, these protective, controlling behaviors have become automatic and habitual. As soon as any fear is triggered, we automatically protect against the fear by arguing, blaming, attacking, judging, shutting down, resisting, or giving in. In relationships, the fears of rejection and engulfment – of losing the other or losing ourselves – generally underlie our protective behavior.

In a relationship, if one or both partners are closed, protected, controlling, then they cannot emotionally connect with each other. No matter how much time they spend together with candles, wine or expensive lingerie, the connection will not be there when one or both are closed and protected. Ironically, when the intent is to get love or avoid pain, what we create is a lack of love and much pain. Our intent to control brings about the very things we are trying to avoid with our controlling behavior.

Our own intent is the one thing we do have control over. We do not have control over another's intent to be open and loving, but we do have control over our own intent to be open to learning about what it means to be loving ourselves and to others. However, it takes both people being in the intent to learn for partners to emotionally bond.

If both are open to learning, then they will be emotionally available to each other and can bond with a touch, a smile, or a kind word. Bonding has to do with the energy between them, not with anything external like candles, and the energy comes from their intent. A controlling intent creates a heavy, dark, hard, closed-hearted energy, while the open-to-learning intent creates a light, soft, open-hearted energy.

The big challenge in relationships is to stay open to learning about loving. Because we automatically and unconsciously revert to our protective, controlling behavior in the face of fear, being open to learning needs to be a conscious choice. Developing the ability to make a conscious choice regarding your intent is a learning process. The hallmark of higher consciousness is being able to choose your intent every moment, even in the face of fear.

When relationship partners are both able to reliably choose to be open to learning about loving themselves and each other, they create a sweet and safe environment for their love to flourish. Then candles, vacations, and lingerie can enhance their experience with each other – the icing on the cake.

Easy ways to bond? Staying conscious and open to learning is not easy! The concept is simple, but doing it is far from easy. Yet devoting yourself to learning to stay open to learning in the face of fear may be the most fulfilling and rewarding experience in your life!

Build a Romance Bridge

Ever run into a brick wall, so to speak, with your partner? Cannot seem to pass "Go" without collecting 200 fresh wounds? Well, it is time to build a bridge and tear down that brick wall. Here are your tools:

ATTITUDE – Get an attitude adjustment first. Lighten up and do a 180-degree about face. Read the Sunday comics, grab an old comic book, turn on the Comedy channel, watch funny videos or DVDs. Get in a better mood and pass it along to your partner. Invite your mate to tune in to comedy with you, too.

FRIENDSHIP – Go back to being friends for starters now that you are in a good mood. Forget the love stuff, if you want. And just focus on being good friends; share compliments, do things for one another, go out and have fun together, enjoy one another's company.

RELAX – Let your hair down. Trust and relax. Be yourself. Do not let old wounds open or fester. Forget the garbage memories and just be in the here and now together.

TIME OUT – If possible, spend extra time together for a while, like during your original courting days. Hire a sitter, order out, eat at fast food places, grab ice cream cones, and go for walks in the park. Get to know each other all over again. That is the key. Then you will remember why you fell for each other in the beginning and history will hopefully repeat itself.

COMMUNICATION – Take it slow and easy. Keep away from subjects that you do not agree upon. And slowly re- learn to communicate with each other all over again. If necessary, and it is not a crime or shame – get help. Seek a trusted friend or adviser, a church clergy member or certified professional counselor. No need to go it alone. Find your weak areas and how to overcome them and plan for future communication difficulties.

GOALS – Gradually develop goals together so you will have a direction to head. Write them down in a notebook just for the two of you. And over time, develop them, revise them, cross them off your list. The idea is to HAVE goals together and work towards a common goal.

SCRAP BOOK – Create a memory album together. Add photos, clippings, menus, and anything that reminds you of the "good times." Then when tough times comes, you will have something to "hold on to" – your bridge to romance.

So do not just sit back and sulk. Take short steps to improve your relationships and let life's problems magically pass by while you hold on to your relationship.

Communication in Romance

Romance. Can it be discussed? It must be experienced, isn't it? But, let us talk of romance, because we cannot avoid discussion about it. Let those in love, decide how correct is this discussion on communication in romance.

Romancing is not a science, but an art. When you talk to your beloved, you talk not only with your words, but with your eyes and your body language. Everything takes part in communication with your sweetheart.

Does one convey love every single day? What and how does one communicate while romancing? Yes, it is true that most of the romantic lovers talk only of positive things and avoid everything negative. It is also true that talk is mostly about love, because they are romancing. It is true that the couples dream of great things and avoid contemplating any negatives.

Romance is different. In romancing there is no place for anything that may kill the mood. Romance means talking of moon, and not the sun. But you can talk of sunsets. Romance does not think about the fate of fallen flowers, but only admires the beauty of flowers smiling on the branch. The world already has innumerable problems, and romance is much needed to create a positive atmosphere in any relationship. Romance is a dream.

Why do Women Get Attracted to Married Men?

The hooked and booked man is like a forbidden temptation. That is what makes him irresistibly attractive to a woman. He stirs a challenge in her. She feels a sense of power in attracting a man who is already taken. What makes him the catch for her is his confidence, experience, and authority. The excitement stems from the fact that he is already taken.

The golden rule here is: you want what you cannot have. Soon, this man becomes an overwhelming obsession for a woman. I call it the 'forbidden fruit obsession'.

According to me, there are two reasons for women falling for married men. Firstly, wild attraction. And secondly, vulnerability. For a woman, a married man represents a certain security she craves. A woman feels that a married man - compared to a bachelor - can meet her emotional and material needs in a better manner. Getting a married man signifies a triumph of one woman over another woman. He is a trophy catch. To have him, is about making the impossible.

If a woman wanted a fling, she could have had it with

anybody. But a married man at her beck and call makes her value herself more... that he is willing to throw it all over for her. It increases her self-esteem. Mind you, she is enjoying this fantasy, as much as his wooing, his experience, and the way he makes her feel extra special.

Sometimes, she likes the fact that he does not go weak in the knees in front of her. He is a symbol of authority. This relationship is about adventure and fun. But this is dangerous fun. There is a risk of running another person's life.

Married men love playing games. They give out the vibe - 'I'm married but I'm game'. Married men are always on the lookout for fun. These are men on the prowl. For a woman, it might be difficult to resist the vibes of attraction from a married man. He makes himself so indispensable.

A married man can give a woman a great time. There are times when this forbidden attraction transforms into love and romance, especially if the man does not have a happy marriage. Not all married men are jerks, some even leave their wives and get married to women they love. But the fact is, men and women love playing power games with each other. This is a dangerous game. It can take a woman and a man through highs and lows, like you have never experienced. Human beings are fragile and one learns from trial and error. So, it is you must decide, whether it is a viable option to have a relationship if you are a married man, thing of the consequences as well.

The Psychology of Long-Term Attraction

The psychology of long-term attraction intricately weaves together a myriad of factors that contribute to the sustenance and enrichment of romantic connections over time. While the initial spark of attraction may ignite the flames of romance, it is the underlying psychological dynamics that fuel the longevity and depth of a relationship. Let us embark on an immersive exploration of the multifaceted aspects that underpin long-term attraction:

At the core of long-term attraction lies Attachment Theory, a seminal framework that posits how early experiences with caregiver's shape individuals' attachment styles, thereby influencing their ability to form and maintain relationships later in life. A secure attachment style, characterized by trust, comfort with intimacy, and effective communication, lays the foundation for enduring attraction and relationship satisfaction.

Proximity and repeated exposure emerge as pivotal catalysts in fostering long-term attraction. The mere exposure effect elucidates how individuals tend to develop preferences for familiar stimuli, including those they frequently encounter. Over time, familiarity breeds comfort and affection, nurturing a sense of closeness and connection that sustains attraction.

Shared experiences and cherished memories serve as building blocks for emotional intimacy in relationships. Couples who engage in meaningful activities, share laughter, and create lasting memories forge stronger emotional bonds that deepen over time, fueling the fires of long-term attraction.

Mutual respect and understanding emerge as fundamental pillars upon which enduring attraction is built. Couples who value each other's perspectives, support one another's goals, and navigate conflicts with empathy and compromise cultivate deep emotional connections that endure the test of time.

Emotional intimacy, characterized by openness, vulnerability, and mutual support, emerges as a cornerstone of long-term attraction. Couples who feel safe expressing their deepest thoughts and feelings forge profound connections that evolve and deepen over the course of their relationship journey.

Physical intimacy and affection play indispensable roles in sustaining attraction in long-term relationships. Regular expressions of love, such as cuddling, kissing, and holding hands, release oxytocin and dopamine, fostering feelings of closeness and connection that nourish enduring bonds.

Resilience and adaptability emerge as essential qualities for navigating the challenges inherent in long-term relationships. Couples who weather life's ups and downs together, supporting each other through adversity, cultivate bonds that grow stronger with each trial they overcome.

Shared values and goals provide a sense of alignment and purpose, fostering lasting attraction. Couples who share core values such as honesty, kindness, and respect, and work together towards common aspirations, experience greater satisfaction and deeper connection in their relationship.

Continuous growth and development serve as catalysts for sustaining long-term attraction. Couples who prioritize personal and relational growth, challenge each other to learn and evolve, and celebrate each other's achievements, cultivate a dynamic and fulfilling partnership that evolves over time.

Effective communication emerges as the cornerstone of enduring attraction. Couples who communicate openly, honestly, and empathetically build trust, resolve conflicts constructively, and maintain emotional closeness, nurturing a bond that grows stronger with each shared conversation and connection.

In essence, the psychology of long-term attraction

encompasses a rich tapestry of psychological factors, including attachment, familiarity, shared experiences, mutual respect, emotional intimacy, and resilience. By consciously cultivating these elements within their relationship, couples can sustain and deepen their attraction over time, fostering enduring love, and fulfillment that transcends the passage of years.

13 CONCLUSION

Seduction is something that both men as well as women undertake to get their partners to have sex with them. However, it is the men who must seduce the women most of the time. The reason for this is that most women feel that men should initiate seduction. This is the reason why every man must learn the different techniques of seduction so that they can successfully seduce any women that want.

Always remember that you need to understand how the women tend to think so that you can create a successful plan of seduction for her. Seduction is a risk if you want to seduce a woman whom you have just met or a woman whom you do not know very well. Give her your full concentration and always act cool and calm. If she senses
that you are nervous then your seduction plan would fail miserably.

Confidence and smartness are the two things that women look out for in men. If you are smart as well as confident then you have a high chance of successfully taking her back to your home. The way you act, balance and talk are also very important. Make her feel that you are a gentleman by doing everything that a gentleman would do. However, try not to be an extremely nice guy otherwise you may end up being her friend. Be nice but act like a little mysterious so that she would become interested in you.

After reading this book, you should put the techniques to practice in order so that you can master the art of seduction soon.

"Seduction Techniques" for the Winners

Imagine that you are already in your college days and still you cannot find a date. Or even asking someone for a date is a misery for you. In short, you find it hard to approach women and lacks confidence in yourself.

Seduction Science in this new millennium are on the rise. Seduction techniques can greatly help guys who find it hard to get the women they always wanted. So, it is not a social taboo anymore. Seduction as thought by many is not wrong in modern society. You are just simply studying the best techniques that will make dating and picking up easier. Seduction techniques are simply getting to know and basically mastering the proper ways of attracting women.

But seduction techniques are not just for men. It is most useful for women as well. These are the women who have been waiting to get noticed by their special men. Well, it is indeed nowadays, a perfect help that life has to offer. Not that it is offering easy tactics on how to collect men or women – but making it easier to enjoy life and find that perfect mate by developing these skills.

Seduction techniques are commonly practiced by people who are not well skilled in terms of attracting the opposite sex. Not that they are unattractive, but are usually shy and therefore there are people need seduction techniques to boost their self-esteem and develop confidence in their selves.

Seduction techniques can also be very helpful in businesses. Like for example, you are a car salesman. And you find it very hard to approach prospective clients. You are wasting your time and effort on studying how to deal with them when you can make business with them. Seduction technique is one great help. You would not imagine how it can greatly affect your sales by simply practicing the principles used in seduction techniques.

Job seekers can also benefit from seduction techniques. While on interview, you can mesmerize the interviewer with the tactics that you have learned by studying the seduction techniques. Not that you are inviting them to indulge into sexual activities, but you can impress them with the way you are boosting yourself. Seduction techniques can tame any roaring beasts.

Seduction technique in general is an absolute solution for men and women who possess low self-esteem, job seekers and even businessmen. People who are in immense need for help, in terms of capturing the hearts of the people they always wanted will be overwhelmed if they discover the wonder of the so-called seduction technique.

So go, and share the seduction technique with your friends whom you know are suffering from different encumbrance in their lives. You can absolutely be of great help in solving the miseries of their own lives.

Finally, if you have found the information beneficial, kindly leave behind an honest review of this book on Amazon.

Your thoughts and opinions are highly valued.

Wishing you the very best,
Don Giovanni